52 WEEKS OF
GRATITUDE & AFFIRMATIONS

GRATITUDE
JOURNAL

Weekly Gratitude Diary
5 minutes a day to reflect on the
good things in your life

CREATED BY
PAPER + BIRD PRESS

PAPER + BIRD

www.paperandbirdpress.com
@paperandbirdpress

Sometimes things go wrong. If you have any problems with the print quality of your book, please email us on hello@paperandbirdpress.com and we will get a replacement copy sent out to you immediately.

What is a gratitude journal?

A gratitude journal is simply a way to reflect on all of the good things that are going on in your life.

There are so many benefits to cultivating a daily gratitude practice...

1. It builds your feelings of closeness, connection and happiness.
2. It has been proven that focusing on positive thoughts gives you a surge of feel good chemicals and improves your mood.
3. Regular journaling about the good things in your life can help when life gets tough and challenges come your way.
4. It can improve your relationships with important people in your life.

How to use your gratitude journal

Starting a new journaling habit can be tough. The joy of this gratitude journal is that you only need to think of as little as 1 - 3 things each day that you are grateful for.

This book is split into 52 weeks where you can reflect on those things that you are grateful for each day, decide what affirmations you want to focus on each week, what has brought you joy this week and what you are looking forward to next week

When you are running low on ideas, you can check the gratitude prompts at the beginning of the book to give you inspiration.

Start small if you are struggling to find things that you are grateful for... the smile of a child, the unconditional love of a pet, the passing aroma of a flower that you walked past on your way to work. Embrace the magic of the small moments in your day to day life and reflect on the joy that they bring.

Commit to your daily practice

Decide that you are going to make a commitment to yourself that you will write something down every day that you are grateful and thankful for.

Choose a time of day that you can regularly check in, reflect on the things that have happened and make your notes on these pages.

Create the space and time for you to give this gift to yourself.

"It's not happiness that brings us gratitude

brings us gratitude

it's gratitude that brings us happiness"

ANONYMOUS

Gratitude Journalling FAQ's

What do you do if you aren't feeling grateful?

If you don't feel grateful for anything in the moment, that's okay - just write a sentence or two about something good that happened recently.

Use one of the prompts in this book to remember a time that you felt good and happy.

This is a way of appreciating something in our lives, even if we are not in the right headspace right now to feel grateful for our immediate situation.

Alternatively, if you really don't feel good today, put the journal down. Do something that makes you feel good and then come back to it, sometimes a bit of space can make a world of difference.

What kind of things should I write?

There is no right answer for this! Some people find gratitude journals effective when there is some kind of prompt which you will find on the following pages, where others find gratitude journals effective when they are able to list all of the things that make them happy about their day in one go.

It's different for everyone, so experiment and see what works best for you.

When should I write in my gratitude journal?

Choose a time that feels right for you. It can be a lovely way to start your day or a way to reflect on the day that has just been. It's your journal to complete your way.

Final thoughts

Your gratitude journal is an opportunity to focus on the good in your life.

It can also help you get out of a negative mindset and improve your mood, relationships, health or finances.

Remember that it doesn't have to be perfect; just write for 5 minutes each day about one thing that happened during the day which made you happy or grateful.

Even if things were terrible all day long (which they sometimes are), try to find something good because there's always a silver lining to be found in every situation.

Gratitude Prompts

1. What is something that you really like about yourself?
2. What is something good that you have been able to do recently?
3. What is something good that happened in your life in the last year?
4. What is a wonderful memory that came up for you today?
5. Who makes you smile?
6. What is something that made you laugh?
7. What did someone say to you today that felt good?
8. What is something that you learned today?
9. What is a small moment of pleasure that you had today?
10. Who are you grateful for in your life?
11. What is something that you are looking forward to?
12. What can you do that you are grateful for?
13. What is a special talent that you have?
14. What has made a difference in your life?
15. Who can you always count on?
16. What community are you really glad to be a part of?
17. What is a piece of music that you love?
18. What is one good thing that happened today?
19. What is something wonderful about your home?
20. What is something wonderful about a member of your family?
21. Has someone done something kind for you today?
22. Did something make you think a happy thought?
23. Where is a lovely local place that you love to visit?
24. What's your favourite food?
25. Who is someone that you appreciate today?
26. Who is someone that appreciates you?
27. Who makes you feel good whenever you are with them?

Gratitude Prompts

28. What is your favourite holiday destination?

29. What piece of clothing makes you feel amazing?

30. What is your favourite feature about your personality?

31. What is your favourite part of your body?

32. Who is someone from your past that you are glad to still be in touch with?

33. What do you love about the work that you do?

34. Who do you enjoy working with?

35. What is one of the traits that you love most about your partner?

36. What is something you are looking forward to today?

37. What is something exciting you have coming up soon?

38. What is something that you feel lucky to have?

39. What is your favourite place in nature to visit?

40. What do you love doing with your friends?

41. What is something useful you have learned that you use in your everyday life?

42. What regularly brings you joy?

43. What is a happy childhood memory that you have?

44. Who is someone that changed your life for the better?

45. What's a skill that you have that you are grateful for?

46. What is something that you look at with love every day?

47. What is something that you love to do just for fun?

48. Where is your favourite place to eat out?

49. What do you do to relax?

50. What smells do you really love?

51. What is something that pleasantly surprised you?

52. What is a challenge you overcame in your life?

53. Who has had a positive impact on your life

54. Who makes you laugh?

today I am grateful for...

monday

....

....

....

tuesday

....

....

....

wednesday

....

....

....

thursday

....

....

....

friday

....

....

....

saturday

....

....

....

sunday

....

....

....

"We can only be said to be alive in those moments when our hearts are conscious of our treasures."
THORNTON WILDER

dates:

....

weekly affirmations:

....

....

....

....

....

....

things that have brought me joy this week:

....

....

....

....

things I'm looking forward to next week:

....

....

....

....

notes:

....

....

....

....

....

today I am grateful for...

monday

....

....

....

tuesday

....

....

....

wednesday

....

....

....

thursday

....

....

....

friday

....

....

....

saturday

....

....

....

sunday

....

....

....

"Good friends, good books, and a sleepy conscience: this is the ideal life"

MARK TWAIN

dates:
....

weekly affirmations:
....
....
....
....
....
....

things that have brought me joy this week:
....
....
....
....

things I'm looking forward to next week:
....
....
....
....

notes:
....
....
....
....
....
....

today I am grateful for...

monday

....

....

....

tuesday

....

....

....

wednesday

....

....

....

thursday

....

....

....

friday

....

....

....

saturday

....

....

....

sunday

....

....

....

"So many books, so little time"
FRANK ZAPPA

dates:
....

weekly affirmations:
....
....
....
....
....
....

things that have brought me joy this week:
....
....
....
....

things I'm looking forward to next week:
....
....
....
....

notes:
....
....
....
....
....
....

"They say a person needs just three things to be truly happy in this world: someone to love, something to do, and something to hope for."

TOM BODETT

Someone that I am grateful for every day is .... *because ...*

today I am grateful for...

monday

....

....

....

tuesday

....

....

....

wednesday

....

....

....

thursday

....

....

....

friday

....

....

....

saturday

....

....

....

sunday

....

....

....

"May you live every day of your life"
JONATHAN SWIFT

dates:
....

weekly affirmations:
....
....
....
....
....
....

things that have brought me joy this week:
....
....
....
....

things I'm looking forward to next week:
....
....
....
....

notes:
....
....
....
....
....
....

today I am grateful for...

monday

....

....

....

tuesday

....

....

....

wednesday

....

....

....

thursday

....

....

....

friday

....

....

....

saturday

....

....

....

sunday

....

....

....

"Remember to look up at the stars and not down at your feet"

STEPHEN HAWKING

dates:
....

weekly affirmations:

....
....
....
....
....
....

things that have brought me joy this week:

....
....
....
....

things I'm looking forward to next week:

....
....
....
....

notes:

....
....
....
....
....

today I am grateful for...

monday

....
....
....

tuesday

....
....
....

wednesday

....
....
....

thursday

....
....
....

friday

....
....
....

saturday

....
....
....

sunday

....
....
....

*"Whatever you appreciate and give thanks for will
increase in your life"*

SANAYA ROMAN

dates:

....

weekly affirmations:

....

....

....

....

....

....

things that have brought me joy this week:

....

....

....

....

things I'm looking forward to next week:

....

....

....

....

notes:

....

....

....

....

....

....

today I am grateful for...

monday

....

....

....

tuesday

....

....

....

wednesday

....

....

....

thursday

....

....

....

friday

....

....

....

saturday

....

....

....

sunday

....

....

....

"When we focus on our gratitude, the tide of love rushes in"

KRISTIN ARMSTRONG

dates:
....

weekly affirmations:
....
....
....
....
....
....

things that have brought me joy this week:
....
....
....
....

things I'm looking forward to next week:
....
....
....
....

notes:
....
....
....
....
....
....

"Walk as if you are kissing the Earth with your feet."

THICH NHAT HANH

the people that I most appreciate most in my life are:

today I am grateful for...

monday

....
....
....

tuesday

....
....
....

wednesday

....
....
....

thursday

....
....
....

friday

....
....
....

saturday

....
....
....

sunday

....
....
....

"God gave us the gift of life, it is up to us to give
ourselves the gift of living well"

VOLTAIRE

dates:

weekly affirmations:

things that have brought me joy this week:

things I'm looking forward to next week:

notes:

today I am grateful for...

monday

....

....

....

tuesday

....

....

....

wednesday

....

....

....

thursday

....

....

....

friday

....

....

....

saturday

....

....

....

sunday

....

....

....

"If you want to find happiness, find gratitude"

STEVE MARABOLI,

dates:
....

weekly affirmations:

....
....
....
....
....
....

things that have brought me joy this week:

....
....
....
....

things I'm looking forward to next week:

....
....
....
....

notes:

....
....
....
....
....
....

today I am grateful for...

monday

....

....

....

tuesday

....

....

....

wednesday

....

....

....

thursday

....

....

....

friday

....

....

....

saturday

....

....

....

sunday

....

....

....

*"Gratitude bestows reverence.....changing forever
how we experience life and the world"*

JOHN MILTON

dates:
....

weekly affirmations:
....
....
....
....
....

things that have brought me joy this week:
....
....
....

things I'm looking forward to next week:
....
....
....

notes:
....
....
....
....
....

today I am grateful for...

monday

....

....

....

tuesday

....

....

....

wednesday

....

....

....

thursday

....

....

....

friday

....

....

....

saturday

....

....

....

sunday

....

....

....

"I may not be where I want to be but I'm thankful
for not being where I used to be"

HABEEB AKANDE

dates:

....

weekly affirmations:

....

....

....

....

....

....

things that have brought me joy this week:

....

....

....

....

things I'm looking forward to next week:

....

....

....

....

notes:

....

....

....

....

....

"When you do things from your soul, you feel a river moving in you, a joy."

RUMI

A challenge that I overcame that changed my life forever was:

today I am grateful for...

monday
....
....
....

tuesday
....
....
....

wednesday
....
....
....

thursday
....
....
....

friday
....
....
....

saturday
....
....
....

sunday
....
....
....

*"I think that real friendship always makes us feel
such sweet gratitude"*

STEPHEN KING

dates:

....

weekly affirmations:

....
....
....
....
....
....

things that have brought me joy this week:

....
....
....
....

things I'm looking forward to next week:

....
....
....
....

notes:

....
....
....
....
....
....

today I am grateful for...

monday

....

....

....

tuesday

....

....

....

wednesday

....

....

....

thursday

....

....

....

friday

....

....

....

saturday

....

....

....

sunday

....

....

....

"Gratitude is the ability to experience life as a gift"

JOHN ORTBERG

dates:

....

weekly affirmations:

....

....

....

....

....

....

things that have brought me joy this week:

....

....

....

....

things I'm looking forward to next week:

....

....

....

....

notes:

....

....

....

....

....

today I am grateful for...

monday
....
....
....

tuesday
....
....
....

wednesday
....
....
....

thursday
....
....
....

friday
....
....
....

saturday
....
....
....

sunday
....
....
....

"When you express gratitude for the blessings that come into your life,
it not only encourages the universe to send you more"

STEPHEN RICHARDS

dates:

....

weekly affirmations:

....

....

....

....

....

....

things that have brought me joy this week:

....

....

....

....

things I'm looking forward to next week:

....

....

....

....

notes:

....

....

....

....

....

....

today I am grateful for...

monday

....

....

....

tuesday

....

....

....

wednesday

....

....

....

thursday

....

....

....

friday

....

....

....

saturday

....

....

....

sunday

....

....

....

"Even the smallest tender mercy can bring peace
when recognized and appreciated"

RICHELLE E. GOODRICH

dates:

....

weekly affirmations:

....
....
....
....
....
....

things that have brought me joy this week:

....
....
....
....

things I'm looking forward to next week:

....
....
....
....

notes:

....
....
....
....
....
....

"Sometimes your joy is the source of your smile, but sometimes your smile can be the source of your joy."

THICH NHAT HANH

The teacher that made the biggest difference in my life was...

today I am grateful for...

monday

....

....

....

tuesday

....

....

....

wednesday

....

....

....

thursday

....

....

....

friday

....

....

....

saturday

....

....

....

sunday

....

....

....

"If we want to keep the blessings of life coming to us, we must learn to be grateful for whatever is given"

HAROLD KLEMP

weekly affirmations:

....
....
....
....
....

things that have brought me joy this week:

....
....
....
....

things I'm looking forward to next week:

....
....
....
....

notes:

....
....
....
....
....
....

today I am grateful for...

monday

....

....

....

tuesday

....

....

....

wednesday

....

....

....

thursday

....

....

....

friday

....

....

....

saturday

....

....

....

sunday

....

....

....

*"When it comes to life the critical thing is whether you take
things for granted or take them with gratitude"*

GK CHESTERTON

weekly affirmations:

....

....

....

....

....

....

things that have brought me joy this week:

....

....

....

....

things I'm looking forward to next week:

....

....

....

....

notes:

....

....

....

....

....

....

today I am grateful for...

monday

....

....

....

tuesday

....

....

....

wednesday

....

....

....

thursday

....

....

....

friday

....

....

....

saturday

....

....

....

sunday

....

....

....

"Each day give thanks for the gift of life. You are blessed"

PABLO

dates:

....

weekly affirmations:

....

....

....

....

....

....

things that have brought me joy this week:

....

....

....

....

things I'm looking forward to next week:

....

....

....

....

notes:

....

....

....

....

....

....

today I am grateful for...

monday

....

....

....

tuesday

....

....

....

wednesday

....

....

....

thursday

....

....

....

friday

....

....

....

saturday

....

....

....

sunday

....

....

....

*"Thankfulness creates gratitude which generates
contentment that causes peace"*

TODD STOCKER

dates:

....

weekly affirmations:

....

....

....

....

....

....

things that have brought me joy this week:

....

....

....

....

things I'm looking forward to next week:

....

....

....

....

notes:

....

....

....

....

....

"When a new day begins, dare to smile gratefully."

STEVE MARABOLI

The most magical experience that I have had in my life was...

today I am grateful for...

monday

....

....

....

tuesday

....

....

....

wednesday

....

....

....

thursday

....

....

....

friday

....

....

....

saturday

....

....

....

sunday

....

....

....

"Gratitude for the seemingly insignificant—a seed—
this plants the giant miracle"

ANN VOSKAMP

dates:
....

weekly affirmations:
....
....
....
....
....
....

things that have brought me joy this week:
....
....
....
....

things I'm looking forward to next week:
....
....
....
....

notes:
....
....
....
....
....

today I am grateful for...

monday
....
....
....

tuesday
....
....
....

wednesday
....
....
....

thursday
....
....
....

friday
....
....
....

saturday
....
....
....

sunday
....
....
....

*"Courtesies of a small and trivial character are the ones which strike
deepest in the grateful and appreciating heart"*

HENRY CLAY

dates:
....

weekly affirmations:
....
....
....
....
....
....

things that have brought me joy this week:
....
....
....
....

things I'm looking forward to next week:
....
....
....
....

notes:
....
....
....
....
....
....

today I am grateful for...

monday

....
....
....

tuesday

....
....
....

wednesday

....
....
....

thursday

....
....
....

friday

....
....
....

saturday

....
....
....

sunday

....
....
....

*"Once gratitude is expressed, it changes attitude, brightens
outlook, and broadens our perspective."*

GERMANY KENT

dates:
....

weekly affirmations:

....
....
....
....
....
....

things that have brought me joy this week:

....
....
....
....

things I'm looking forward to next week:

....
....
....
....

notes:

....
....
....
....
....
....

today I am grateful for...

monday

....
....
....

tuesday

....
....
....

wednesday

....
....
....

thursday

....
....
....

friday

....
....
....

saturday

....
....
....

sunday

....
....
....

"I see the glass half full and thank God for what I have."

ANA MONNAR

dates:
....

weekly affirmations:
....
....
....
....
....
....

things that have brought me joy this week:
....
....
....
....

things I'm looking forward to next week:
....
....
....
....

notes:
....
....
....
....
....

"Acknowledging the good that you already have in your life is the foundation for all abundance."

ECKHART TOLLE

A time that I remember that always brings joy to my heart is ...

today I am grateful for...

monday

....

....

....

tuesday

....

....

....

wednesday

....

....

....

thursday

....

....

....

friday

....

....

....

saturday

....

....

....

sunday

....

....

....

"Gratitude brings JOY and laughter into your life
and into the lives of all those around you"

EILEEN CADDY

dates:
....

weekly affirmations:

....
....
....
....
....
....

things that have brought me joy this week:

....
....
....
....

things I'm looking forward to next week:

....
....
....
....

notes:

....
....
....
....
....
....

today I am grateful for...

monday

....
....
....

tuesday

....
....
....

wednesday

....
....
....

thursday

....
....
....

friday

....
....
....

saturday

....
....
....

sunday

....
....
....

"Joy is the simplest form of gratitude"

KARL BARTH

dates:
....

weekly affirmations:

....
....
....
....
....
....

things that have brought me joy this week:

....
....
....
....

things I'm looking forward to next week:

....
....
....
....

notes:

....
....
....
....
....
....

today I am grateful for...

monday

....

....

....

tuesday

....

....

....

wednesday

....

....

....

thursday

....

....

....

friday

....

....

....

saturday

....

....

....

sunday

....

....

....

*"Acknowledging the good that you already have in your life is the
foundation for all abundance"*

ECKHART TOLLE

weekly affirmations:

....

....

....

....

....

....

things that have brought me joy this week:

....

....

....

....

things I'm looking forward to next week:

....

....

....

....

notes:

....

....

....

....

....

....

today I am grateful for...

monday

....

....

....

tuesday

....

....

....

wednesday

....

....

....

thursday

....

....

....

friday

....

....

....

saturday

....

....

....

sunday

....

....

....

*"The art of being happy lies in the power of
extracting happiness from common things"*

HENRY WARD BEECHER

weekly affirmations:

....
....
....
....
....
....

things that have brought me joy this week:

....
....
....
....

things I'm looking forward to next week:

....
....
....
....

notes:

....
....
....
....
....
....

"If the only prayer you said was thank you, that would be enough."

ECKHART TOLLE

spending time with these people brings joy to my life

today I am grateful for...

monday

....

....

....

tuesday

....

....

....

wednesday

....

....

....

thursday

....

....

....

friday

....

....

....

saturday

....

....

....

sunday

....

....

....

"Gratitude turns what we have into enough"

ANONYMOUS

dates:

weekly affirmations:

....

....

....

....

....

....

things that have brought me joy this week:

....

....

....

....

things I'm looking forward to next week:

....

....

....

....

notes:

....

....

....

....

....

....

today I am grateful for...

monday
....
....
....

tuesday
....
....
....

wednesday
....
....
....

thursday
....
....
....

friday
....
....
....

saturday
....
....
....

sunday
....
....
....

*"Gratitude is a powerful catalyst for happiness. It's
the spark that lights a fire of joy in your soul"*

AMY COLLETTE

dates:
....

weekly affirmations:

....
....
....
....
....
....

things that have brought me joy this week:

....
....
....
....

things I'm looking forward to next week:

....
....
....
....

notes:

....
....
....
....
....
....

today I am grateful for...

monday

....

....

....

tuesday

....

....

....

wednesday

....

....

....

thursday

....

....

....

friday

....

....

....

saturday

....

....

....

sunday

....

....

....

"Gratitude makes sense of our past, brings peace for today, and creates a vision for tomorrow"

MELODY BEATTIE

dates:

....

weekly affirmations:

....

....

....

....

....

....

things that have brought me joy this week:

....

....

....

....

things I'm looking forward to next week:

....

....

....

....

notes:

....

....

....

....

....

today I am grateful for...

monday

....
....
....

tuesday

....
....
....

wednesday

....
....
....

thursday

....
....
....

friday

....
....
....

saturday

....
....
....

sunday

....
....
....

*"Gratitude is when memory is stored in the heart
and not in the mind"*

LIONEL HAMPTON

dates:
....

weekly affirmations:
....
....
....
....
....
....

things that have brought me joy this week:
....
....
....
....

things I'm looking forward to next week:
....
....
....
....

notes:
....
....
....
....
....

"When we give cheerfully and accept gratefully, everyone is blessed."

MAYA ANGELOU

the music that makes me feel good is...   and here's why ...

today I am grateful for...

monday

....

....

....

tuesday

....

....

....

wednesday

....

....

....

thursday

....

....

....

friday

....

....

....

saturday

....

....

....

sunday

....

....

....

"Gratitude is happiness doubled by wonder"

GK CHESTERTON

dates:
....

weekly affirmations:
....
....
....
....
....
....

things that have gone well this week:
....
....
....
....

things that I'd like to improve next week:
....
....
....
....

notes:
....
....
....
....
....
....

today I am grateful for...

monday

....

....

....

tuesday

....

....

....

wednesday

....

....

....

thursday

....

....

....

friday

....

....

....

saturday

....

....

....

sunday

....

....

....

"You only live once, but if you do it right, once is enough"

MAE WEST

dates:

....

weekly affirmations:

....

....

....

....

....

....

things that have gone well this week:

....

....

....

....

things that I'd like to improve next week:

....

....

....

....

notes:

....

....

....

....

....

....

today I am grateful for...

monday

....

....

....

tuesday

....

....

....

wednesday

....

....

....

thursday

....

....

....

friday

....

....

....

saturday

....

....

....

sunday

....

....

....

"Good friends, good books, and a sleepy conscience: this is the ideal life"

MARK TWAIN

dates:

....

weekly affirmations:

....

....

....

....

....

....

things that have gone well this week:

....

....

....

....

things that I'd like to improve next week:

....

....

....

....

notes:

....

....

....

....

....

today I am grateful for...

monday

....

....

....

tuesday

....

....

....

wednesday

....

....

....

thursday

....

....

....

friday

....

....

....

saturday

....

....

....

sunday

....

....

....

"So many books, so little time"

FRANK ZAPPA

dates:
....

weekly affirmations:
....
....
....
....
....
....

things that have gone well this week:
....
....
....
....

things that I'd like to improve next week:
....
....
....
....

notes:
....
....
....
....
....
....

"Pursue what catches your heart, not what catches your eyes."

ROY T. BENNETT

the best holiday I ever had was...

today I am grateful for...

monday
....
....
....

tuesday
....
....
....

wednesday
....
....
....

thursday
....
....
....

friday
....
....
....

saturday
....
....
....

sunday
....
....
....

"May you live every day of your life"

JONATHAN SWIFT

dates:

....

weekly affirmations:

....

....

....

....

....

....

things that have gone well this week:

....

....

....

....

things that I'd like to improve next week:

....

....

....

....

notes:

....

....

....

....

....

....

today I am grateful for...

monday

....

....

....

tuesday

....

....

....

wednesday

....

....

....

thursday

....

....

....

friday

....

....

....

saturday

....

....

....

sunday

....

....

....

"Remember to look up at the stars and not down at your feet"

STEPHEN HAWKING

dates:

....

weekly affirmations:

....
....
....
....
....
....

things that have gone well this week:

....
....
....
....

things that I'd like to improve next week:

....
....
....
....

notes:

....
....
....
....
....
....

today I am grateful for...

monday

....
....
....

tuesday

....
....
....

wednesday

....
....
....

thursday

....
....
....

friday

....
....
....

saturday

....
....
....

sunday

....
....
....

"Whatever you appreciate and give thanks for will increase in your life"

SANAYA ROMAN

dates:

....

weekly affirmations:

....

....

....

....

....

....

things that have gone well this week:

....

....

....

....

things that I'd like to improve next week:

....

....

....

....

notes:

....

....

....

....

....

today I am grateful for...

monday

....

....

....

tuesday

....

....

....

wednesday

....

....

....

thursday

....

....

....

friday

....

....

....

saturday

....

....

....

sunday

....

....

....

"When we focus on our gratitude, the tide of love rushes in"

KRISTIN ARMSTRONG

dates:

....

weekly affirmations:

....
....
....
....
....
....

things that have gone well this week:

....
....
....
....

things that I'd like to improve next week:

....
....
....
....

notes:

....
....
....
....
....

"Find time to stop and thank the people who make a difference in our lives."

JOHN F. KENNEDY

the most wonderful thing happened this month which was...

today I am grateful for...

monday

....

....

....

tuesday

....

....

....

wednesday

....

....

....

thursday

....

....

....

friday

....

....

....

saturday

....

....

....

sunday

....

....

....

"God gave us the gift of life, it is up to us to give ourselves the gift of living well"

VOLTAIRE

dates:

....

weekly affirmations:

....

....

....

....

....

....

things that have gone well this week:

....

....

....

....

things that I'd like to improve next week:

....

....

....

....

notes:

....

....

....

....

....

today I am grateful for...

monday

....

....

....

tuesday

....

....

....

wednesday

....

....

....

thursday

....

....

....

friday

....

....

....

saturday

....

....

....

sunday

....

....

....

"If you want to find happiness, find gratitude"

STEVE MARABOLI,

weekly affirmations:

....
....
....
....
....
....

things that have gone well this week:

....
....
....
....

things that I'd like to improve next week:

....
....
....
....

notes:

....
....
....
....
....

today I am grateful for...

monday

....

....

....

tuesday

....

....

....

wednesday

....

....

....

thursday

....

....

....

friday

....

....

....

saturday

....

....

....

sunday

....

....

....

*"Gratitude bestows reverence.....changing forever
how we experience life and the world"*

JOHN MILTON

dates:
....

weekly affirmations:
....
....
....
....
....

things that have gone well this week:
....
....
....
....

things that I'd like to improve next week:
....
....
....
....

notes:
....
....
....
....
....

today I am grateful for...

monday

....

....

....

tuesday

....

....

....

wednesday

....

....

....

thursday

....

....

....

friday

....

....

....

saturday

....

....

....

sunday

....

....

....

*"I may not be where I want to be but I'm thankful
for not being where I used to be"*

HABEEB AKANDE

dates:
....

weekly affirmations:

....

....

....

....

....

....

things that have gone well this week:

....

....

....

....

things that I'd like to improve next week:

....

....

....

....

notes:

....

....

....

....

....

....

"When you are grateful, fear disappears and abundance appears."

ANTHONY ROBBINS

a memory that I will cherish forever is...

today I am grateful for...

monday

....
....
....

tuesday

....
....
....

wednesday

....
....
....

thursday

....
....
....

friday

....
....
....

saturday

....
....
....

sunday

....
....
....

*"I think that real friendship always makes us feel
such sweet gratitude"*

STEPHEN KING

dates:
....

weekly affirmations:
....
....
....
....
....
....

things that have gone well this week:
....
....
....
....

things that I'd like to improve next week:
....
....
....
....

notes:
....
....
....
....
....

today I am grateful for...

monday

....

....

....

tuesday

....

....

....

wednesday

....

....

....

thursday

....

....

....

friday

....

....

....

saturday

....

....

....

sunday

....

....

....

"Gratitude is the ability to experience life as a gift"

JOHN ORTBERG

dates:

....

weekly affirmations:

....

....

....

....

....

things that have gone well this week:

....

....

....

....

things that I'd like to improve next week:

....

....

....

....

notes:

....

....

....

....

....

....

today I am grateful for...

monday

....

....

....

tuesday

....

....

....

wednesday

....

....

....

thursday

....

....

....

friday

....

....

....

saturday

....

....

....

sunday

....

....

....

"When you express gratitude for the blessings that come into your life,
it not only encourages the universe to send you more"

STEPHEN RICHARDS

dates:
....

weekly affirmations:

....

....

....

....

....

....

things that have gone well this week:

....

....

....

....

things that I'd like to improve next week:

....

....

....

....

notes:

....

....

....

....

....

today I am grateful for...

monday

....

....

....

tuesday

....

....

....

wednesday

....

....

....

thursday

....

....

....

friday

....

....

....

saturday

....

....

....

sunday

....

....

....

"Even the smallest tender mercy can bring peace
when recognized and appreciated"

RICHELLE E. GOODRICH

dates:

....

weekly affirmations:

....

....

....

....

....

....

things that have gone well this week:

....

....

....

....

things that I'd like to improve next week:

....

....

....

....

notes:

....

....

....

....

....

....

"There is a calmness to a life lived in gratitude, a quiet joy."

RALPH H. BLUM

reflections:

reflections:

reflections:

reflections:

reflections:

PAPER + BIRD

www.paperandbirdpress.com

@paperandbirdpress

hello @paperandbirdpress.com

Printed in Great Britain
by Amazon

35883591R00076